D1563184

MADONNA OF THE CELLO

Madonna of the Cello

POEMS BY *Robert Bagg*

WESLEYAN UNIVERSITY PRESS
Middletown, Connecticut

Some of these poems have previously appeared elsewhere. Grateful acknowledgment is made to the editors of the following: *Massachusetts Review, New Poems by American Poets No. 2* (Ballantine Books), *Poetry, Transatlantic Review, Audience,* and *Voices.*

Quotation from *The Autobiography of W. B. Yeats* (Part Two of this book) copyright © 1916, 1936 by The Macmillan Company, copyright © 1944 by Bertha Georgie Yeats, and used by permission of The Macmillan Company.

Lines by William Butler Yeats (Part Four of this book) from *The Collected Poems of W. B. Yeats,* copyright © 1928 by The Macmillan Company and used by their permission.

Library of Congress Catalog Card Number: 61–6972
Manufactured in the United States of America
First printing February 1961; second printing December 1962; third printing December 1967

for John Moore

CONTENTS

PART ONE

Her wraithful turnings and her soft answers head
    Me off. The easiest allusion of her hips,
No matter how well spoken for, soon slips
    Her mind. I ask her long blonde braids where they
        lead,

Hold them over her head, and let them fall.
    Even her breasts' tactfully gathered favor
Can't hold my hand's attention forever.
    Lazy as her love is, I have my hands full

With her, letting every beauty she owns
    Slip through my tongue and fingers, still hoping
For the whole of her, soon closing and opening
    Like a giant heart toying with my bones.

The Gorges of the Loup

She sat winded, her eyes watered, and her blouse
Filled and eased after the long climb from Grasse.
Her tears had touched off half-laughing hiccups
Which she quieted with deep painful gasps.
Snail tracks led past her nose to bright poised shells
Moved by how far we'd come from our first troubles.
I thought: I am not beauty's champion,
Not for this ailment. She is on her own.

A witch with no more right to live than perfume
Shadowed us. She will make sense of the bloom
When life for the lupine turns untenable;
Fog-nosed March mountains lie amenable
To her wand's touch. A climber's second wind
Is her gift too, so is farsight, and all mind-
Expanding self-appraisal she inspires.
On the lookout for that witch, we sensed the river's
Drunken sculpturing of limestone, followed
In sober detail by a mountain road.
The Gorge below heightened this morning's drizzles
Into hundreds of surefooted waterfalls.

Under her fluffed-out skirt, lavender and thyme
Sparkled her relaxing undercurves. How come
The casual pleasure and sunny confusion
Of her life, now schooled in concentration
By mute hills and white ricocheting water,
Secreted so much sadness whenever
Her mind wandered from her eyes?
                                        Jasmine stills
Refined the hillside's lackadaisical smells.
I admired her eyes as uncanny wanderers
That have a grip on all things except tears.

4

You changed clothes for the party in my room,
And when your laugh got muffled in the costume
Pulled past your crinolines, I saw that terror,
Joy, like a tight becoming gown, grip and lure
You on, holding your moving curves to their longing.
I knew you would conceive my child that Spring.

Fresh from thousand-flowers some invisible bees
Idled by. But no happening could please
Both her and me, that evening on the mountain.
Some memory her heart failed to hold in
Ached through her body. Maybe too much milk
Was ready in her breasts. She looked at the long walk
Down, dreamed how dizzy the rhythms of the trail
Slaloming toward the valley would make us feel.

She looked as though her tears were left over
From the first time she came, and made me wonder
If there were any better way than this
To bring pain powerfully condensed, across
Years to her face, pebbled now as if with sweat.
I was reminded of a winded athlete,
Of a warrior lighting into his fury
Or a storyteller working off a story.

Her thriving pupils opened their needle's eyes
To the world's richness, which entered them with ease.
But sunlight let go of us and unearthed stars.
Varied airs closed our pores and cracked our ears
Clean, as we ran down the mountain in cold shoes
And the smell of lavender in our clothes.

Antlers of black lightning
Illumine the stag's rude head,
His perfectly teamed
And rising forelegs.
When he hits, the lit land
Crackles with black bone.

Water he came down to drink
Freezes like a stalked animal.
Stormclouds mill in its stillness.

The heavens welcoming storm
Are welcomed by his thirst:
His snout drains the mirror
Of its impounded violence,
The progress of the storm
Pauses in his poised body.

His hooves go lording
In the lake's salaam, salaam,
His head rises to a tomahawked
Brandish of his conceit:

The storm must spume
First from his nostrils.
In one second more,
Against a background
Of blundering crescendos
And rain letting down abruptly
As suspended disbelief,
He snorts.

Muscles eddying at cross
Purposes in his flanks
Align, and focus
In his four hooves,
The body he threatened to share
With the plunging heavens he takes back
In one bound, he crashes

Black under the overcast
And loud over the underbrush.

Paolo and Francesca

On the shoulder of the road,
 In a buzzing halo of bystanders.
Black tire marks, rubbed off an eye-wrenching screech,
 Lead up to them: in their eyes
The remains of astonishment whistles over
 Jackknifed spines, over places in their necks,
Stomachs and elbows where blood they still breathed
 Oxygen into, slides
 Imperturbably into the world.
The way her knees tuck to her chin, her skirt
 Rumples loose past her hips, his fingers
 Seem lost in her blouse, rich sleep-matted
Hair half-hiding the open agony of her mouth, you'd
 think
 Someone had caught these lovers
In the act and separated them by brute force.
 By his kneeling a Franciscan
 Breathes in God to be blamed.

But there is nothing to keep them from being
 Paolo, with Francesca
Riding sidesaddle on his Lambretta, her arms
 Hooped round his loins,
Blowing out of Rome's rush hour, his wrist
 Twisting more and more gasoline into
Elaborate collaboration with the cylinders,
 Aspiring through three gears
 To dead calm on the straightaway,
Nothing—but the tail end of a Fiat flicked them:
To their lightheaded hair, skidding smiles,
 An ancient archway
 Opposed its stone.

8

A white sheet settles, billowing
　　Ease over their jagged figures.
I cannot believe the Franciscan's
　　Mechanical Latin does much good
　　　　Toward the proposition that:
These tangled bodies rooted in this earth
　　Flower somewhere.

Nor will he be content
　　How I see them off,
　　　　Forever relying on
The pressure on his pulse
　　Of the expectant eyes
　　　　Of the girl about to come
　　As gasoline—
Happy thighs close on the body's
Acceleration into blood.

Ronald Wyn

Inscriptions on Greek tombstones intrigued him,
The way stones spoke to the dead with sure words.
'This little stone, good Sabinus, records
Our great friendship, which I still need. Leave the
    numb
Waters of Lethe alone, and remember me.'
Sometimes the dead answer, 'Please don't worry
Long over me. Do your work, be happy. At nineteen
Cancer killed me, and I leave the sweet sun.'

We both had strong Platonic appetites.
Three-pound symposiums of grapes and plums
Gnawed bare to their Aristotelian pits
He pocketed. 'Logic thrives on a peach blossom's
Troubles,' he said, and when a calm mirror
Lake reflected us, we dove underwater,
Blew out mouthfuls, and swam until the honey
Of exhaustion filled every cell in the body.

From a frame normally tense and careless
A tennis ball exacted gracefulness
By skipping on the tip of the net's tongue.
The dust kicked from our reflexes in long-
Winded rallies. Sharp satisfying plocks,
Both of us bent on keeping play alive,
We'd silence with a winning forehand drive,
Let sweat cool, and drink harsh gulps from our
    Cokes.

His death ten seconds in my ears, I shook
Off sorrow, walked out in a cool downpour
And drank rain from my palms. I had no power,

So thirsty for his slippery life, to make
Anything but absurdity of that bath.
I wandered Amherst in drenched shame
Because I had let weather drive the same
Wonder from my feelings as a man's death.

This Spring, at Epidaurus, dying of poems,
I stood tired and sweaty in a great cloudburst.
Only for honest, singleminded thirst
Will sense be made from the skies by cupped palms,
Said the acoustics in this theater, where
Greek speech lives cupped in the worn marble's care.
I shall drink many palmfuls of my friend's life
In your presence, laurel and myrtle leaf;

Then set these stones speaking to each other.
'I am Ron Wyn, promising philosopher,
I pledged myself to music, calculus
And Greek, but mastered none, since my last
    promise,
To death, was the one I fulfilled first.'
'Rest easy, Ron. Although our friendship was killed
To metaphor by the illiterate world
I grave these rocks with love, in which you are
    versed.'

The Risen Eyelid

I was very tired when we arrived in Algeciras,
And I wandered tired, looking for a room to rest in for some
   hours.

The one I found was on the ground floor of a courtyard,
And as I lay in the impatience of exhaustion, waiting for sleep,

Two children in the palms outside found something that pleased
   them,
And hit it over and over with Spanish words like little fists.

They tired of the thing first hit upon, but found others, and at
   last
Found each other, and kept shouting Joselito! Maria!

Shouting so tirelessly I carried these names
Deep into sleep with me, as one carries a mild headache,

Valuable as something always there to take up when we wake.
But when I awoke there was no headache or throbbing of names,

The courtyard was quiet with darkness, and as refreshing
As a mind with no memory, on which the first thing it touches

Happens forever: A girl with inevitable black hair
Striking her comb through it with practiced violence,

Turning her head white-eyed as she heard my door crack open,
The strands escaping to their uncomplicated destinies.

PART TWO

Adventures

> *I now can but share with a friend my thoughts and*
> *my emotions, and there is a continual discovery*
> *of difference, but in those days, before I had*
> *found myself, we could share adventures.*
> WILLIAM BUTLER YEATS

Flight from Reichert's Backyard

When Reichert struck paired fingers at the prop
The engine sparked up, sputtered, and conked out.
He spit, then returned his arm to the rhythm
Of an aching unlucky wand. But one
Offhand downbeat could fill that cylinder,
The size of a lark's lung, with pulsating
Alcohol. Tinkering and exhilaration.
Sparkplugs were switched, batteries charged, coils
Flushed with doctored gasoline. Half-hearted
Flutterings almost blurred to one solid roar.
I knelt by the plane touching her tissue wings,
Soaking up twilight released from the same sky
Ascending from the elms which yesterday
Seized our vibrating biplane just as bluely
As a leaf or a robin.
                          I remembered,
How we recoil when the action starts:
The fluted prop flickers invisibly
Into sound. Back drafts buffet McCornack,
Who holds the fuselage like a leopard's tail,
Hair riffling, his shirt puffed like a huge blister.
The roar steps up our whispers to punctured
Shouts as Mac lets go. The plane bobbles along,
Her wheels roll irrelevant to the lawn,
Slack! brings the guy wires taut, she climbs out flat,
Soars in lopsided halos overhead.

But now it wouldn't fly. Sensations of lilac,
Fatigue, were spilled down unimportant nerves,
But itches still danced out of reach. Who had
Three hands? Who didn't need to take a leak?
We slammed the sick prop in gathering anger

Until we were ourselves machinery,
In our ritual ornery as the plane,
Thinking like motors, wishing compression, spark
And pulse of pistons would catch inside us.
The plane sat still: a great big dead damned bird.

Mac's blue irises bloomed as it got dark.
"Somebody get a carbide lantern—Mac!"
"To hell with you." Somebody's thick fist thumped
Somebody's ribs. After that a long lull.
Schemes brewed for liberating the landlocked sun.
Mac cleaned his knife, the rest of us milled, until
A splash followed the *boing* of an expanding
Tin can: Reichert was sowing kerosene pools
Which caught like an idea everyone gets
At once and grew thick skins of hair-raising flames,
Stiff hairs of smoke standing on end. One by
One we turned cartwheels devils might have dared.
Heads singed low, then righted infected with sparks.
Reichert let his burn, I doused mine in damp grass.
Steam rose from waterlogged dungarees,
Dizziness sluiced down semicircular
Canals, spinning spreadeagled the tipsy lot
Of us on the burning lawn, which slid and bucked
A different way for each of us. We crumpled
Foul of each other's shins, stuck with scorched hair,
The public flames, our personal earthquakes—
Magic carpets that would not touch the earth
Ever. But fire wore off, and we came down
On headaches like the Rock of Ages, cleft.
Five of us maneuvered on the charred circle,
Hilarious. The moon's aluminum paint

Soaked eerily through our sleeves and forearms.
Screen doors began slamming and our parents
Panted up after us, shouting our names:
McCornack, who smoke rhododendron leaves,
Reichert, who had a beautiful sister,
Al Farley, with a good eye for the sun,
Charles, who lived on a nearby mountain,
And I, Bob Bagg, stared down once by the sun.
We told our parents lies and stuck to them.
Our sodden bodies lumped home. After dinner
We all had appetites for flight to burn.

I lay in bed over the garage, listening,
Suffering kinks and weary uselessness,
Ready—as night so cleaned the neighborhood
With clarity and quiet the elms and owls
Turned terribly aware of each other,
Tremolos hoots creaks rustlings and sly whirrs:
Animals began feeling out the leaves,
The moon for something dismal in the grass.
I thought of the sun as torn loose and burning,
Barreling toward us like a hurricane
One day off, the radio and static air
Warning us of the foolproof sun, arriving
To show us up.
                    Sparrows near my window
Bore down on stuttering split-second songs
Whose promise quickly petered out. I pushed
Off into sleep, longing for one single
Sailing call, blown long from reeling lungs,
Till what I imagined burned through to what was.
Caws loudened, and showed me a way out of sleep.

I swung up and hung to the window. There
Crouched Mac, ten fingers flared out from his mouth,
Supplying the droll call of the crow.

                              Reichert
Rolled his terse eyes for me to follow him.

The others were clumped in a football huddle
Out behind Reichert's barn. Homing pigeons
Cooed as they were handled, preened in their cage.
"There's one for each of us," Al Farley said,
"You're first." He tossed a bird at me, with bland
Round eyes, slopping wet, stinking kerosene.
From behind me a match scratched, sputtering
Lit past my shoulder. It hit the pigeon
Which caught fire in my hands.

                              "For Christ's sake, guys!"
Was what I must have yelled, fighting to rid
My fingers of it, its ghastly eyes, its wings
Fumbling with flames, its claws contracting on
My forearm. Feathers riffled stench up my nose.
He sat down squat and wouldn't fly.

                              I dropped
Down on him, peeled him loose, but pain stuck fast
To my palms, already gaudy with charred blood.
Flames sewed him in a flimsy orange sack.
I threw a punch at Farley, but he yelled "Look!"
At what was hard to look at as the sun.
At last the urge for air and frenzy drove
Him off the earth. I felt, following him
As he flew, stunning impulses flung out
From my solar plexus—

I love his flight:
Air seized by his wings perfectly useless
To shake fire off him like some abstract curse.
I love the gyros of my eyes following
Flames, love hearing terror evaporate
With his life. Kerosene dries. He burns now
In his own right.
        And I love the raw creature
Caged in the thrashing slush of my stomach,
Sliding back through my guts to the unwinding
Time when man and bird paused: one animal
Minding its pain.
        A long compressed calmness
Blooms me to my limb of creation, which the bird
Fades above as his flames die down: he trails
Feathery embers, a tiny sun forever
Settling into the rhododendrons, leaving
Behind a savage avalanche of darkness
Stoning my eyes.

Death at Pocono Lake Preserve

The lifeguard's parallel simian arms
Paused by his side, then bore down on the boy's back
To teach those lungs a cadence they had known
For years.
           Sometimes his eyelash flickered just
Too delicately for us to glimpse the eye.
He loved playing on our peripheries.
The people on the lawn wept and marveled:
The slight hesitant child had boldly drowned.
He'd roamed the edge of people, animals,
And water, shedding manners like hot clothes.
One afternoon he followed me around
Spitting at my attention, then skipped and ran,
Tugging me like a fitful spaniel
Behind some old abandoned horseshoe pits,
Where a blind dying hound sat in a whir
Of insects, his yellowed tongue unfurling
Like flypaper. The child's eyewater flowed
Faster than he could see through, and I sensed
The hound, the bouncing insects and myself blurring
Into each other. We poked the animal
With sticks, and shooed the flies, but couldn't stand
To see him struggling at standing, like a foal.

With plumes of cotton out his nose, he lay,
And grew a faint grin. We expected him
To put both palms down on that slight left knee
And push himself dizzily to his feet.
We took to running hands over our legs
Watching the child lose color to the tanned sun.
From sitting so long cramped and cross-legged

My right leg fell asleep, and when I shook it
I set up maggot tingles in my nerves.
They carried him pale in a green blanket
Back to the doctor's office, by good fortune
Not fifty yards away. As it got dark
We lay on the damp grass imagining.
"I'd like to see what's going on in there,"
McCornack said. "By climbing on the skylight.
Crash through and I'd land splash on his stomach,
Whoosh all the water out, rise a wet hero."

No word from inside. Night birds nudged the ground.
Occasionally a thrush would drop down hard
And stick, just like a dead ball that won't bounce.
A few at a time people left the lawn.
Stars lighting on and off, dim then brilliant
As fireflies, when my eyes moved in the pines,
Lit up his face thrilled with a mason jar
We'd filled with fireflies caught in our cupped palms.
"Look, we're outside the universe, looking
In," I told him, as those phosphorous bellies
Swelled to their nervous super novae.
I pictured his curious far-off face. Stars
Blinked in the inquisition of his eyes.

When I went to bed later on that night
I tried holding my breath, tried to imagine
Clandestine pleasures of unconsciousness
His eyes would not relinquish to my glower,
And failed. I was self-conscious of his death.
His body floated face down on my dreams.

Mosquitoes touched my arms with a soft tickle
But sucked pain suddenly. I slapped my skin
And smeared wet blood, felt the hard welts of flesh
And grew tired, happy now in heavy sweet
Safeties of sleep I felt chirring overhead.
If only I could feel how it was not
To feel, my nerve ends limp, eyes unillumined,
Nights immersing me in numb black water,
Myself forgetting myself in the blank wash,
But bitterly I warmed to wakefulness
As vague bites localized in fitful points.
I wore my discomforts thin as my skin
Envying him, in whom flies and mosquitoes
Had no interest, pallid of brow and blood,
Whose senses spilled like water off the dam,
Who left me all alone with all this life.

Dead friend, you freed the dim bad bugs of night
Convening now above my bundled head
In terrible skirls and ruined drones.
They all will spend their minutes on my skin
Except your fireflies, live and aloof as stars.

The Sewer Dare

The spring I recovered from pneumonia
Outdoor light hurt my tentative eyelids,
Though painful cardinals and forsythia
Soon opened them for good. From lilac vapor
And honeysuckle, lungs regained eloquence
With their strength. Weather turned warm grace-
    fully,
As though won by a beautiful argument.
Elated by this sweat-provoking sunlight
I took my first cold shower of the year.

Screen doors—pried open rickety—held back
Their slam until I pushed off the top step
Of the porch, staggering under my own weight,
Then ran myself back into condition
Against crocuses, tulips, narcissi,
But found that nature set a killing pace.
Spring drew me on, an enormous incoming
Breath my lungs tried hard to hold, and exhale.

Though left winded by my pursuits, jackrabbits
And butterflies, I seldom could back down
From a human dare.
          To haul ourselves
Hand over hand along telephone wires,
Our biceps shivering with exertion
But our legs scissoring uselessly,
Was one sure way to join Pete Reichert's gang.
Or be electrocuted.
          My stammering
Refusals got pummeled—pugnacious feints
Brought my guard up, but only bottlecaps

Doubled in Reichert's fists. His fingers, which
Flinched when I tapped the hand that struck me
     lucky,
Relaxed, and palmed a Pepsi-Cola cap.

Reichert broke its news gently, busy screwing
That opaque monocle in his eye: "You know
The old storm sewer runs under Sagamore?
We've bellied through it during thunderstorms,
But you guys better hope for decent weather."

McCornack, hunched over his sunken chest,
Volunteered. He had failed to recite
The Lord's Prayer yesterday, while, pinned squirming,
A hen pecked chicken feed off his bare belly.

A Nedick's top whose luck lay untouched, put out
His other eye, then a flourish of his brows
Dropped both the bottlecaps off Reichert's blinding
Zombie stare focused at five thousand yards:
Maybe Nedick's meant Mountain Avenue
Jammed in Charley's buggy, with a running start,
One wheel loose, and Bagg steering with his knees.

By deadpan razzmatazz they tried to squeeze
Chickenhearted arrogance out of me,
Cleverly unravelling my shoelaces.
They limped in spoofery of my sloppy feet,
But my smile fattened on my swallowed pride.
McCornack teamed with me, and the iron grill,
Crowbarred upright, tottered over our fingers.
We let go of the street, the grill clanked shut.

24

Reichert peered through the manhole: "Hey, little
    rain
Coming down." They quieted to let us listen.
Somebody's leak tumbled on the macadam,
Superbly timed. "Bastards, I can still see blue,"
Mac whispered. *Bastards* was fed back to us
Pompously amplified. Reichert's whinneying laughter
Hollowed the sewer out ahead of us.
Unforeseen waterdrops glanced off our spines.
Palms leaving holes slurping in the leaf slime
Left by runaway rainfalls, ghouls of the cold air,
Something to be shrugged off, weighed down our
    necks
With the sewer's imperturbable narrowness:
Constriction of being bound and gagged
Without one enemy rope to fight against.
When we saw no sense could deal with raw dark
Our jitters settled down into this coolly
Echoing costume, shriveled to all fours.
We wormed the way a jointed finger does,
In the finger of a glove.
                    When open-eyed
Blindness put the same hysterical pressure
On our pulse as swimming underwater, breath
Held prisoner in our lungs and our suppressed
Hearts working up a tremendous racket,
We had to come up for air pretty soon,
Or breathe against the wishes of the sewer.
My fingers circling both McCornack's ankles
Rattled him. My thighs loosened and my neck

Ligaments eased. I nursed a match. Mac's eyes
Broke out in the dark looking shame at me,
A shambles from trying to shake the slimy
Feel of salamander footprints off his fingers.
With the stunned sureness of a thrill from some-
Where near the balls lighting into my spine,
Water soaked through my trousers, a drenched hand
Fondling my stomach, followed by a shallow
Curdle in the ears, keen along my shins.
Water rose under us, squeezed from our drizzling
Kidneys and cloudbursting imaginations.

Mac tried to pivot and crawl back the same way
We came, but his buttocks jammed his forehead
Flush against stone. His thin bones in his clothes
Grappled and winced, under the spell of a cruel
Peristalsis. We fought, swallowing hard,
Up that throat like things we didn't want to say.
Stuttering *shits* collided in my larynx.
How could we get the Mississippi off our necks?
McCornack's knees hunched for Pete Reichert's
        crotch.
Take it easy I kept saying, we're going to die.
I dreamed of Reichert trying to sit tight
On our bodies, remembering us as swollen
Blobs of pain burbling through his abdomen.
Arrowheads, candles, friends, underwent foam;
My sister's curls danced in a sodden languor
Below me, caught in the world's strangest wind.
I couldn't hear a word my mother called
From our porch, which floated out of my mind.

Sometimes, when stone barricades met my nose,
Auroras unclenched their colorful fingers,
But soon the fiery hand that palmed me turned
To clammy stone. That all darkness secretes water
Is knowledge I was steeped in, then forgot
In the wash of courage running out on me.

A steady pulse of water flushed our faces,
Then the flood passed. Nozzles of garden hoses
Bumped our kneecaps. Sunlight fell through the
    manhole
As Reichert and his buddies pried it off.
It was the biggest swindle of our lives.
Our thoughts, clenched on ticklish fireflies of light,
Opened upon the overwhelming sun,
Which I got used to, climbing the stems of hoses
Toward the blue manhole-shaped heavens. A sar-
    castic
Hush stiffened some shadowy rhododendrons.
My eyes seeped out of hiding, welcome as
Dampness climbing through the lush complexion
Of a crocus. When I came to my senses,
There, towering in a human pyramid,
Was Reichert's roaring gang, topped by Reichert
Rollicking in his personal glory.

He gathered a huge breath out of the sky.
"Those beauties don't even know they're alive,"
He trumpeted—and for weeks after the word
Death seeped into our foreheads, then dried out
In sunlight and breezes of a day like this.
We stood sullen, each trailing a live hose.

Rearing out of his gang on two uneasy
Knees, Reichert offered fists doubled on air,
But the pyramid collapsed under him,
Some hopeless with laughter, others tripped up
By their shoelaces, none worse than Reichert
Slumping down in satisfied exhaustion
Drenched to his skin. For once I had a good grip
On water, blown out a limber nylon hose.

Cynthia and Abigail arrived breathless
And sandyeyed, a bedspread's tassels pocking
Their cheeks, just too late to see what happened.

Love unravelling with a spider's vigor
In some damp corner of a sleeping porch
Was my lightest industry in a sad mood.
I let it spin so willfully frail
It never ceased tickling the lips of girls
Hurrying and my rivals feeling their way
Through soft cobwebs, cruel and caressingly torn.
A girl sorry she was busy went briskly off
About her business, many moons away.
Insults I smiled through ripened slowly,
Playful smacks in the teeth which leave no pain
But numbness, anger numbed as I mumbled
Slovenly past the lump building in my lip.

Bicycles and big cars in a hurry
Hissed across wet pavements, *Ivanhoe's* huge
Pages turned in the slow wind of the story.
Rebecca's long patience and risen passion
Knead Hebrew balm through Ivanhoe's ragged
Christian muscles: *These will heal in eight days.*
But his chain mail hangs like an old man's skin,
Her dark beauty lies buried in a mirror.

Beside the ballads from my radio,
Heartbroken, but not telling the half of it,
Angelfish making love in a wobbly bowl
Reminded me of white hands caressing
Flimsily, soft whorls never interlocked.

Strange hunting horns entered the telephone's
Ring: Reichert's sigh slyly entrenched itself
In my receiver, and sucked at my thoughts.

I warmed the mouthpiece with swelling longbows;
Towns ringed with crenellated whistles;
How unicorns must canter on the lookout
For the dead giveaway of a chaste pulse.
His listening seemed to siphon these things
Into his own enthusiasm: "Ivanhoe,
We're taking off soon as the rain dies down."

Lithe off her velvet windowseat, thundersqualls
Trying the patience of the river Don,
While two gay men labored her future, coming
Slowly to swordspoint, Rebecca slipped out,
Her steps churning her hem to an insistent
Surf edging upstairs, though up higher her thighs
Hardly moved. Slow as honey in April
She neared my hammock. I stretch—this majesty
Must dishevel—but my eyes marl with cool
Whitelash and saltsmart after her hips swerve,
Skirts following with a reluctant flair
Down a lane my eyes opened through the drizzle.

Once outside, I caught up to them winded.
A stone in each palm, Reichert stalked an oak
Whose flickering squirrels mocked the quickness
In his reflexes. The oak inched slowly
In Reichert's way. He'd learned to wing with his
Left hand, the month his right arm knit in a sling.

Rockbottom swearwords lobbed plump through the door
Of an oldtimer's mountainside bungalow
Brought him out after us cracking a bed slat
Right and left. When his sweaty lenses slipped

Enormous eyes shriveled. Could hardly run,
My body felt all daydream below the waist.

We stretched out in the crotch of a capsized oak.
After each cool swill and swallow, black cola
Exploded foam above Mac's adam's apple.
He handed me the fizzing half-filled bottles.
Caffeine and sugar worked such outrageous
Energy loose from our sloshy insides,
Not even Reichert came up with a scheme
Desperate enough for our stepped-up hearts.
We milled down bridle paths at a dog trot
Willing to meet all happenings halfway,
Swivel-hipped through saplings, broad-jumped dead
    logs,
Our lungs pumping us lazily uphill,
Down dale to the depths of our diaphragms.
When honeysuckle stitched steps together, worse
Than crossed shoelaces, gradually we gave in
To the green tendrils. I broke their fragrance
Open, and sucked. Mac lit a rhododendron curl,
Puffed it. Farley lay dead. Reichert admired
The day's last stronghold of light: a lookout
Summerhouse of a log pagoda style,
Wide open to the valley but guarding
The shilly-shallying of green pinafores.
A shy face at a time, it flushed with girls
Glumly listening, occasionally
Mimicking the fun birds had with their voices.

We'll have it to ourselves, soon they'll be gone.
Shadows wore the Hills-going-nowhere away.
Under some green rustling rhododendrons

Salamanders drank water through their skins.
How come wind roused, and by opposing magic,
Rain saddened me? Rain I can drink, but all
Wind is imagined, that was the answer.
Disgusted air plumped Reichert's cheeks, then
    thrummed
His sinuses. "Guys, a Unicorn snort."
We made a bad but resounding job of it.
Dooot-dooo. Dooot-dooo. Long tapering cries.

"Somebody's fooling round out there, Miss Brown."

We held our howls and chirrups just long
Enough to put a solemn momentum
Into the quiet Reichert raised with his hand.
Whipped overhand, a fist of dirt left Reichert's
Fist sizzling dirtsmoke off its hazy flight—
Battered dust detonated when it hit.
Another, shot from Farley's catcher's peg
Sent mice fragments skittering under skirts.
Miss Brown took charge, but she tried alternate
Policies of hollering and disdain.
We laid down a tremendous bombardment
On well-built girls and broomstick ones alike.
Miss Brown elected to abandon ship.
"Don't panic girls, walk right by, right on by."
The trail downhill led right between our legs.
"No funny business from you gentlemen."

"Us Unicorns aren't no gentlemen, ma'am."

All of a lilting, look-what's-happening
Mood, girls lined the rail, holding themselves dear.
But out they came, in a long safari line,
Inching their way down the trail, holding hands
From toehold to toehold, performing coolly
With the hill's steepness gripped in their puckered eyes,
Half-hoping their hold on themselves would let go,
We figured, sure the hill was on our side.
One blonde flounce seemed to slip on her own laugh,
A squealing landslide broke from Miss Brown's care,
Airing spine-tingling legs and lengthening braids,
Wild and safe, till honeysuckle where we were,
Standing crouched to catch them scrambling by,
Slurred their speed. They played into our hands a game
Of two-hand touch, ouch on their sunburned backs,
The thump and spill of body contact sport.

Reichert's knife flashed, a girl commanding two
Preposterous pigtails one bound up on him.
Some gave in early, were harried cartwheeling.
Petulant white calves pedaled from somersaults.
As I gained, knitting shoulderblades beat
Beneath her blouse. I wished she would take off
And fly, but I whacked where she suddenly
Was. Tomboy knocked out of her, she collapsed
Ladylike, yawned, pretending eight hours sleep.
I shook her spit off. Our breath came easier
Kneeling awed, as for a dead animal.
She rearranged her hips, and crooked a knee,
Her dress took forever sliding down it.

She sneered at the good look I got of her,
Watching me realize what a prize I held,
How much she weighed, and how that weight would
    work.
Well, she said, you have a long way to go,
Instinctively as a maiden statue
Lingering her hand over soft female hair.
All blood descending from my consciousness
She moulded with her gentle chilly hands.
There must have been great sweetness in her, to let
A sharply perched mosquito draw his fill
Of blood, before she slapped him to her neck,
But why she never used such blood, or my hard
Exhilaration which belonged to her,
She never said, only, You're wonderful
Just the way you are. Then left, dizzily
Guiding the brambles past her hair, walking
Lightly, as if everything had happened.
I tried humoring four unruly Cokes
From my kidneys, then Reichert manned the dusk
Highstepping through honeysuckle, a girl's
Ponytail flopping from his hip pocket.

Hallowe'en

My strides balanced the easy swing in my arms.
Water in gutters kept me company
But drained excitement from these streets, now
        calmed
By many elms, and the blink of owl-eyed homes
Through the rasping branches. A surly child
Counted her candy cross-legged on a lawn
Hopelessly overrun with moonlight. I
Howled by, her hand pushed a spellbinding crone
Off her face, hard candy cracked under molars.

Imagination be a witch tonight
Who has on hand a leper's thumb, a hank
Of white hair, footstealth of Japanese snipers,
Quick-witted lizards with languid poisons,
Ladies in locked rooms woken by a knock.
Stir these throughout my smouldering body,
Idle witch, turn more comely as you stir.

Reichert is kneeling under our noses.
With luminous green lines he chalks a nude
On the sidewalk. Strokes pursuing her hair
Down her back follow where her belly leads.
Curves taken in by her fanciful breasts
Embolden into buttocks. But Reichert's still
Unsatisfied.
          "I say scratch the scrub hair
On her neck. She'll feel your hand from then on
Coming on . . ." The punch line to his story stayed
Up in the air, palpably as the time
He hightailed it down the mountain, a girl's
Ponytail flopping from his hip pocket.

35

"Look out for their ribs, they tense when they gig-
   gle."
"How about hips?"
                              "Hips are important, but—"
The firmness of Reichert's sculpturing hands
Made believe air had innocence and had sweat—
"Nipples and slippery thighs are sure fire."
Whole neighborhoods were tossed past our shoulders
In a tremendous spirit of conquest.

The brutal undeclared war within us
Was won. Love-philtres brewed deep in the glands,
Bratty flatchested girls with hopeless calves,
Whipped into shape by their own eyelashes,
Ruled our faux pas *with RSVP eyes.*
Carolyn, Alice, and Mary Anne bobbed up,
Slippery as apples. I bobbed for their cheeks,
A toothless wonder. Sniffs of their shampooed hair
Under my nostrils as we danced, their thighs
Fearful, back pedaling in pedal pushers
As I pursued them down delaying rhythms,
Always were brushing against what perilous
Modesties clothe the beauty in the blood.

Five hundred yards in to our second winds
Our lope collapsed, down to a ramshackle walk.
Our ruddy exhilaration was worn down
To room temperature by an oak fire.
We crashed the party. All the loosest girls
Lolled on the arms of chairs, lulled by mulled cider.
A scissoring rearrangement of legs
Made room among the gently warming wallflowers
For us, who'd brought in fresh ice to be broken.

Mary, whose bosom was famous for bubbling
Loose from her blouse last summer, stunningly
     tanned,
Her skirt crushed in great handfuls, her balance lost
To the rough and tumble of the undertow,
Yawned now if a boy's eyes worried her blouse,
Back of her hand hiding a gaudy smile.

Bones sulked under the stairwell, his last year's
Girl powdering upstairs, making up her mind.
Barefoot, counting stairs with her toes, she came
     down.
"Hello, Bones. Where's your sexy sophomore
     bunny?"
But later she kissed his lips as a mother
Kisses the place where her child burned himself.

Moths flittered through a jack o'lantern's eyes
And out his smile, but dozens of blinded
Couples contracted in darkness, top-heavy,
Sleepily happy. Unasked girls and the stags
Squirmed in ghastly pools of conversation.
If I cut in, some girl would pull herself
Against me, cure my passion at her pleasure
I supposed, in that infuriating darkness.

Farley's elbow moved Anne's angora breast
But tension in her forearm kept him off.
Later she had a headache, ran upstairs
With two other girls, reappeared in the kitchen
Leaning against her original date.
That wasn't what I wanted, some sweet thing

Contracting like a snail I'd touched with salt
When I pulled her toward me out of some song.
If I'd had pride, I'd have cleared out of there,
But a wish for the whole moving presence,
From temporary curls to soft upper knees
Of a girl, kept me staring with my courage
Balancing like an uneasy supper
In the callous depths of my abdomen.
I wrestled with some fist fight in a schoolyard
Years ago: puffed lips, gravel-slashed kneecaps,
Both of us bloody, nobody so cowardly
To imagine a reason why we fought.
She is why, that girl there. The thump of fists
Thumbed on the bass viol, and saxophones cooled
Male anger to temperatures she could use.

Idyllic acid ate away at me.
My palms grew slick, a fist closed in my throat
On eloquence I hoped to win her with.
Maid Marian, what happened to that gown
Of Lincoln green, what do you wear nowadays?

My hand reached somebody's entrenched shoulder,
A boy came loose from his girl. Stunned, almost
Left naked she seemed. Then a warm blues rhythm
Came over her. I sensed myself climbing,
The impending downward swish of a soap-
Box racer tingling in those uphill trudgings,
A climbing until everything falls away—
Toboggan runs down rumpled mountainsides
With the white world bellying up at me,
Streets, shining with icy playfulness, unmoved

By spirited Cadillacs kicking slush,
Homes anchored by parents and furnaces,
Girls cutting angels in the virgin snow.

In that whoosh of cheeks ripening in the wind
I got higher and higher on my own blood,
But nothing fell that Hallowe'en.
                                        Although
She had knotted her arms around my neck
As if counting one hundred against an elm.

'Laine

Where Lackawanna's tracks graze our backyards
An elm opens toward its leaves. Slight wooden slats
Climb its trunk crazily like vertebrae
To my old tree house, house of three girls, all
Named 'Laine.
               'Laine unafraid listened for diesels
Scaring 4:39 out of our watches,
Diesels rattling our wrists, the elm tree's slats,
And a half-mile of track. Faces flicked past
Like faces on a riffling deck of cards.
Our eyes wrinkled after a college girl
Sipping gin in the club car. "Your wife for sure,"
'Laine said, thumbtacking the Black Queen of Spades
(Pulled deftly from the deck on her first try)
Beside DiMag. "You'll marry her on Friday
And spend the morning swimming in Bermuda,"
She whispered, spreading down cards like sandwich
    halves,
Perhaps shuffling herself deeper in the deck.
She looked in my eyes as if they led somewhere,
Then spread my palm, and until dinnertime
Ran her ball-point pen down my life's blue rivers.

Two nights before school ended, wondering if
The elm house still would hold us, we climbed there,
Twisting uncomfortably close together
Since there was truly only room for one.
"This is how lovers stretch," she said, arranging
Copper hairpins like fireflies in her hair,
"Their twin hearts click as tracks click beneath
    trains,
Their eyelids whir out of sight in no time."

She counted three times over my twelve wild ribs.
Soft felt roosters crowing in her green dress
Folded away, trackless and white her thighs
Lay side by side, her lips closed over mine,
Closed bitterly, then opened by my ear.
"You've followed me where all the meagre rivers
Overflow my eyes, sailed so far downstream
The ocean when you reach it, is a wide lie.
If you think schooners beach on gentle islands,
You'll surely founder in my furious hair."
She curled toward nonexistent blankets, and her
Arms cooled as winds breathe gooseflesh over water.
"When you and Charles go overseas this summer
Other girls will beckon from their speeding berths,
Their sheets will rise like crests, but I'll stay here
Traveling warm nights on waves that never break."
A spring of woven roosters settled on
Her ankles, as she alighted from the elm.

Though the vast church is draughty, though the
    pews
Absorb these vows, organ music will insist
Oaken doors swing open on the same spring
That's flourished since the ceremony began.
Skin that once held her breasts high as her bra
Now holds them, cools below her wedding gown,
And later on tonight will shiver at
The first disastrous passing of the diesel,
She will search old trails blazed through civilized
Flesh, itch for woolen summers when shrill roosters
Sang from green fences piled past waking waists.
How shall her voice close over our whole lives?

"Our wedding night was several falls ago,
Now spring comes wearily on a cold scent
With perfect confidence, that foxes bleed,
That snow will find its way to waterfalls,
That if our eyes soak blurring skies with love
Invisible ink will draw taut warriors
And kitchenware from stars."

                        Tonight, dear 'Laine,
Mysterious threads draw headlong birds to sleep,
The blood flies home by sweetly charted courses.

PART THREE

I met Nausicaä when I was her age,
Tipsy from the sea's throes, nothing on her merry-
Making body but saltwater sparkling dry.
When I left she waved from the water's edge.

I vowed I would settle for no lady less,
But all I got was a statue's stony stare.
And my eyes and nostrils stung by the azure
Shallows Venus shrugs off like a rumpled dress.

Speak This Kindly to Her

The final secret that two lovers shared,
Their tumbling out of love, they kept for days,
Knowing how previous farewells had fared.

Just being patient would not work always,
She said. That took time, and time was better used.
Often, completion of a passionate phrase

Lapsed into breath. At parties their eyes cruised,
Hawks again, not kindly feeding the other's wants.
Soon they grew strangely soulful and amused

Splashing each other with clumsy pleasures, once
Swum in a style anything but debonaire,
Cool masters now of what drowned them once by
    chance.

"The old curl-less way, that's how I loved your hair."
"Your careless praise for it was my first despair."

A Good Night's Sleep

Look what startling disguises
   My friends wear in dreams!
   Venus, stark naked, beams
Behind hornrimmed brown glasses.

Christ smokes, dangling both legs
   In someone's swimming pool.
   He is supremely casual
But his conversation drags.

God has the face of a wild
   Card seen as the deck riffles
   Off my fingers. This baffles
The mountainous eyes of a child.

I

Not far from Elgin's marbles, Marx
Drugs the word *class* to ride roughshod.
Near Byron's *clear, placid Leman*
John Calvin loads the dice of God.

I take aim at these men. They are cold
Adversaries. With no great pains,
Scant research or theology, I
Demolish them in four quatrains.

II

To the head and shoulders of a man
Marx fused the instincts of a horse.
History's pulse is quickened—not
By fullblown Helen—but a fat purse,

He reckoned. But against some wall
Stood those embattled stone sculptures
Of an occasion being risen to.
Marx was a fool to bet on the centaurs.

III

Leman is where uneasy souls
Bathe in a watery suspense,
Half-sunk already. Calvin hedges
Between a past and future tense

To wash down our damnation with.
All night the constellations grind
My judgment out, and I swim and
    work
In starlight, while stars make up their
    mind.

Ezra Pound and Robert Bridges

"We'll get 'em all back," said Robert Bridges—
Apollo, the second person singular,
Borrowed ladies, nightingales, all our outra-
    geous
Tricks of diction, the troubadour's flair
For carefully premeditated song—
So the Laureate, marveling at Pound's coura-
    geous
Archaisms. "The world is singing on one lung.
Well away, lad, may your style be contagious."

Pound gave him the horselaugh. But Philomela,
He knew in his heart, never had it so good,
Her mother tongue ripped out, her true tralala
Decoded bluntly by the reader's blood:
Pursue the Immortal like a passing craze.
Despite slick typestrokes of your Smith-Corona
Compose in the sequence of the musical phrase.
Lo! that vacant balcony in Verona.

Apollo and Daphne

Only a poet could be moved by her nervous
  charm,
He dreamed, but she took Hollywood by storm.
What good is spoken or sexual valor
Once her hair's enhanced by technicolor?
She wished it, though. Sarcastic as the god
Apollo, he watched the screen, chainsmoking,
  crazy
With high laughter. As lithely praying Daphne
Comes true, what can he do but knock on
  wood?

Sustenance

If you starve anything,
A race, a flower, a fever,
Fear it will rise and cling
To you, for you can never
Kill something true for
    good
By cutting off its food.

I knew a sinner once,
God was his meat and
    drink.
He wouldn't look askance
At Christ, or say he shrank
Because the world had
    given
No saints lately to heaven.

Ballad for a Woman of the World

So I might light her cigarette
In frequent cabarets
I courted silly Alouette
Of free and fancy ways.

When I was a green hand at love
She welcomed me in velvet
Soft as skin it sailed above,
Discreet as lakes at sunset.

She slept in sensual dismay
Dashed off by drunk Toulouse,
But woke spark-eyed, and felt her day
Burn toward evening like a fuse.

Crinoline rumors of a lover
Rustled as she waltzed by.
Her lash would open high and hover,
Undressing almost a virgin's eye.

How deeply my eyes focused there
As ragged waltzes dragged me under—
O Goblets, fill with *savoir-faire,*
O Absinthe, make the fond heart
        founder!

And legs! for all your genteel ardor,
Prancing outside her gown
As Gershwin glides along her garter—
You'll never dance that music down.

Sonnet by the Lakeside

She was not beautiful, the water showed.
Water had a way like that, of throwing back
Reflections when it should have fallen clear
To pebbles and the shrug of diving minnows.
No tails led deep that her eyes might follow.
Gently, the riding surface blurred her brow.
Perhaps her features' frail asymmetry
Was nothing more than ripples smiled by swans.

Waves smoothed, but night had glazed her mirror
    dark.
Hung on a hawk's arc, her eyes rode swanless sky.
No white wings beat against her beauty there,
For stars have countenances all their own:
Angular Diana holds aloft the dead bird.
Orion admires quietly the brilliant kill.

Lullaby and Aubade on a Hot Night

Because you drowse and breathe, your hair
    piles
    Over, cottons to your ears
So you don't hear rain, or feel the hills
    Cradling the storm's thunders,

And since your eyes are firmly closed
    Down to their slim horizons
Your blonde eyelands shall be exposed
    To no shock but the sun's,

Which won't come for five hours yet.
    Sleep toward this wish of my arms,
Sally, as if in a hammock, sweat
    And swing in the moon's arms

Till damp sleep sweetens your wakening
    And your eyes go wide as suns yawn.
May moisture cool your skin, and cling
    Your fulness to your nightgown

As your life, steeped in dreams all night,
    From breasts and fingertips, clears
Away all sorrows but this sunlight
    Failing our day-dreaming stars.

Confetti for a Red-haired Bride

Who knows for sure what fails, when faint praise
     falls
For red hairs' wilting fire, settling as ash?
Every ten syllables his lips hesitate.
Once buried, she revives to no one's touch,

But a song once fell asleep and woke a girl.
As if commissioned by the Medici
She stands on stocking feet in the sunset
And fancies he will help her down the stairs

Of this Italian terrace, and off to dinner,
Her hand in his hand, as from their pedestals
Aphrodites from stilted civilizations
Alight to shame the belles of his beau monde.

Lo, long ago one came who remembered
To invoke the magic of being mortal.
This prince once kissed a sleepy antique maiden
Upright out of dreams. He carried her outside,

Past tapestries where intrigues lay unraveled,
Past silken steeds fraying to threadbare nags,
Toward love's sun, where she rose, rode side-saddle,
And died a sibyl once upon a time.

Poseidon and Demosthenes

A man mumbling sorry mouthfuls
   Wanders to the shore, where wan-
      dering
Is a peaceful kind of mumbling.
But shouting through sore mouthfuls

Of pebbles starfish cockle shells
   Makes a great thing of mumbling.
   Hear the sea's mouth mumbling!
Full of pebbles starfish cockle shells.

Proposed Elegy for Jane Elizabeth
Should She Die Young

No bird in a cuckoo clock
However recklessly he sang his cues
Was more fond than you were of the pure emergence.
You swished to the surface with wet hair,
Yellow whorls combed sunstrand narrow by water,
You dove and rose from the lake as easily
As you fell in and out of love.
This afternoon, after all our quarrels and promises
Have sparkled and sprinkled away, your blonde head
Shakes off the waves.

We have chafed our towels against the sunset, and stayed
Looking straight up at the gull-free sky,
Relying for life on your one tumbling curl
That never tired of the breeze.
How I loved this, our warm-eyed and only afternoon,
And now I wish I had loved you more than the after-
    noon.

No matter how shrilly
I whistle back through that stillness
I wake no birds buried deep in the drowsy clock
That they may sing you to the surface.

I always knew the death sleeping inside you
Would awake on a sleepless night,
And wake everyone but you,
That hands would close in on the clock
Unable to hide its face ticking on the edge of tears,
That I would look through a thousand mornings
For my rareblooded bird to flash from her niche.

Dispersed the councils: and the armourers
Search the black sky for sun, to show their
    wares.
Each of us now has left his own house, living
Publicly, largely in the streets, by the falling
Wall, watching the valley brew our invaders.

O lichen-eyed Athené, this work is yours!
Shall the great blast of breath which men
    fallen
In a body shall toss upward, enrich heaven?
Be more satisfactory to your nostrils
Than ripe incense and nineteen perfect bulls?

The bullet tugged at his left sleeve
While shrapnel trilled her farewell prattle.
"So long, Soldier." Could she believe
Feeling would deepen in that battle?

His wound is being cauterized,
Charred black to hold his blood at bay.
As pain is slowly realized
His facial muscles underplay

Hot promptings of the healing steel.
The wound goes black where red steel
    goes,
The nerve ends die like men, and feel
Blood glazing them, as fame heals heroes.

She who fingered this aftermath
Died when his cut was fresh and raging.
Her final smile had cut a swathe
Through that lost battle, and now, aging,

A streak of stale sensation runs
Below the scar's white ghost of harm,
Leaving him something of the sun's,
A woman's touch along his arm.

Her left leg lagged behind her right,
A firm step followed by a limp.
Her pigtails haggled down her neck
Like lines of far-fetched hemp.

I watched the shameless way she
    lamed.
She needn't limp so lumpily,
I thought, so I called down to her,
"Hey, you don't need to limp."

She let her hair have its head—
It went its separate ways—like rope
Let out to trim a coming storm.
She stepped into an easy lope.

King Croesus carried to Apollo's sibyl
    Gifts golden to the core,
Infallible gold shining as her syllables
    Shone: Croesus was fully aware
Truth came highly priced and hard, like war.

He was nervous when she whispered to the god,
    Fumes clouded what he came for.
Blood dozed as his veins inhaled what she said:
    Strike Persia with this war
And dark tears will dry on a dazzling Empire.

Exultant Croesus swung her prophecies
    Like tongue-sharp flanges on his ax.
Enemies toppled to its truth like lies.
    (O Croesus, you were lax
To trust your faulty grasp of Attic syntax.)

That morning all the baffling lines of battle
    Joined like a palindrome.
Reading left he saw his veterans ripple
    Forward like straw in a broom.
Then reading right saw his cavalry crumple.

She Is Brought on Her Wedding Night
to a Regency Bed Still Surrounded
by the Whisper of Scandal

Flames on three candlesticks
Smile quietly as angels
Over these fragrant antiques.
This is our bed, my bride,
This rustle of fragile revels
Whose tenants loved and died.
It's best if no one speaks.
One kiss, and the mood dishevels.
Come lie down, see if the bed creaks
Sighs of kings and demoiselles
Long since hushed to their hells.

See That One?

See that one with tanned arms, nice
   hips,
Joking with the soda jerk?
See how her nipples perk
Out her blouse when she sips
Her soda, and her shoulder slips

Into view when he teases her?
You want to pick her up?
Would you mind her make-up,
How her sentences slur,
Or, curled up in a car, her purr?

Two Ballads from Nausicaä

Am I such a temporary girl,
So thin and uninspiring
And so lightly weight his heart
That he may leave me, and still sing?

Could he have sailed so facilely
If mine were mortal spells,
If passage through my eyes
Were dangerous as Dardanelles?

All I owned were minor faults
Like a tongue too warm and free,
Like lips touched rich with salt
That touched him to his journey.

His journey never was inspired
By anything practical,
Nothing that could be cured
By my being beautiful.

He wasn't carried away by triumph.
Though her eyes might purr with azure
Urges, surely no sultry nymph
Gave him more pleasure.

Those things that I feared early
Turned pliant as my limbs.
Like a hair across his eye,
I lay golden, I lay slim.

But he steered clear of lazy olives,
The hyacinths, and me
And my linen-voiced loves
Toward the longwinded sea.

I must have made him restless
With my eyes drowsy always,
While pale turmoils of my dress
Unnerved him like white lies.

He feared this was too perfect,
Lived only on the tongue,
That we'd tire of its effect
As words tire in a song.

He said I held no harshness,
No iron rhythms to master.
He'd be too mild, unless
He made love to disaster.

Maybe I won't be soft and sure
When you sail off the water,
Maybe perfection can be cured.
Maybe, sailor, I'll be bitter.

Were these eyes not magnificent
To fool, this frightened hair
No trick to soothe and circumvent,
My thighs nothing to beware?

Whatever sleeps inside me
Dreamed too long under your hand.

Words tire in my song,
And I am lonely in a sunny land.

II

The crow lies over the cornfield,
The sun flies over the crow.
The crow will fall on the corn,
The sun will light on the crow.

Fishermen find the water
A surface of sad smooth sounds.
I fished the surf for a sad sad man,
Now he is only sound.

I cleaned his brow of salt and time
With hands of river water.
I wish his hands and luck
Would never run like water.

"Aha," he said, "A glimpse of your hair
Sends shivers throughout the sun.
I swam through death and drenched I rose,
But I will dry in the sun."

With bird-sharp eyes he whistled to me,
Tossed me like grain at the breeze.
The sun sets over his shoulder,
His words go by on the breeze.

The crow lies over the cornfield,
The sun flies over the crow.

66

The crow will light on the corn,
And sun will fall on the crow.

Fishermen find the water
A surface of sad smooth sounds.
I fished the surf for a sad sad man.
Now he is only sound.

PART FOUR

Does the imagination dwell the most
Upon a woman won or a woman lost?
If on the lost, admit you turned aside
From a great labyrinth out of pride,
Cowardice, some silly over-subtle thought
Or anything called conscience once;
And that if memory recur, the sun's
Under eclipse and the day blotted out.
WILLIAM BUTLER YEATS

I

There is this story of a Faery Child:
The Land of Heart's Desire by Willie Yeats,
And all our troubles came because we willed
Upon a tense girl those high-handed traits:
Red hair, a firm calm among all passionates,
A free-wheeling pre-Raphaelite speech,
Could run fast, stood no taller than John Keats,
Had nimble eyes. But she was still a bitch
Because of her wild body she let no one touch.

II

On one side she was fresh and feminine,
But on the other bone wings and vertebrae
Touchingly fluttered underneath her skin.
Her sweaters smelt of woodsmoke, her hair of bay.
We liked her motionless smile, but not the way
We were eluded by her idle speed.
Ralph moved the better, battling for this fey
Girl, being wiry and restrained, though an odd
Word of mine summoning her hair sometimes turned her head.

III

Ralph Lee and I slumped on her kitchen floor,
Our spirits socked in by hopeless ambitions.
"I'm no actress. For that sweaty career
You need too many leered-at emotions."
"Faery Child, we'll scare up some pristine ones."
"Oh, I like the peace of never having any."

71

Just pose for our hands, and pretty soon your skin's
Coolness will flow more famous than Greek honey.
"Don't call me Faery Child. Don't. Makes me feel phoney."

IV

Kissed, she was a pale camellia turning brown.
We dyed her rusty. A curtain's sensual flare
Keyed her up—still, she froze when she went on.
"Isn't your life slipshod enough? Out there
You're Queen. Death wants a good grip on your hair,
You pilot your adrenals, your voice is schooled
By all the speech it swallows. Girl, you won't care
With whose high spirits your stomach gets filled:
Giselle, Blanche Dubois or this crazy Faery Child."

V

Lowering a hearth gently from the heights
We set a Sligo cottage up onstage.
My old mother swears at the fire she lights,
My bride spills daisies from a dreamy rage.
Faery Child knocks, taking soft advantage
Of our quarrel, begs her fill of warm milk,
Then sings my bride to the woods. "Can you manage
That exit in a more Ophelian arc?"
Ralph calls, but she's already gone off in the dark.

VI

She jumped rehearsal for a climbing elm,
By her knees swinging down, wound up and weird,

(Mediterranean makeup whitened by cold cream)
To the nylon limits of her leotard.
Her hand becomes astonished by my fevered
Forehead, as though she found there fresh genius,
Not adolescent lust. What treed her? Had she heard
Distant stanzas giving tongue? She slides down, her face
Chilly as our footsoles through the watery grass.

VII

Crazed at the luck of my ascendency,
Ralph quoted all my wretched verse to her,
Made a chorus of satyrs from *papier maché,*
Our friendship growing hourly more severe.
Envy so sharpened our mornings, we could hear
A girl clear her throat or merely swallow,
And tell if she were fair or a real loser
From that private sound. Hushed in my cool pillow
Tubercular Puccini sopranos coughed hello.

VIII

The flushed young dates in scotch and cha-cha steep,
So tired they can no more keep happiness
From sopping through them than they can keep sleep.
Gone from Phi Psi's corridors the strenuous
Maturing of frank hips: smoke-ring sensuous
Now, girls murmur and drift, subtly breaking
From burial in one boy's hold to delirious
Heaven in his roommate's arms, lazily making
Fun of a fashion they have no intention of forsaking.

Diaphanous posses going after Dionysus
(Harsh flares, black-haired Maenads in dazzling condition)
Set out at midnight up Mount Parnassus:
He leads their toes over moss. Sparse oxygen
Lightens their thoughts. Enormous nervous tension
Tears squirrels, warms brooks and phalloi. Pleasure
Comes letting go of all they came to own.
Girls bundle home over the Notch, their driver
Immersed in soft mists off the Connecticut River.

X

Long after midnight in the Phi Psi house
A drunken instructor's caroling collapse
Rallies some brothers for a final carouse.
His mouth acrackle with potato chips,
Snickers falling on his libidinous quips,
He says, steadying himself on my lapels,
"She gives me willies, Bagg, watching how she slips
Her gloves off. Phi Psi can take piety and scandals,
But not a witch who takes off from your window sills."

X I

"Gould, don't you know anything about Willies?
Much worse than gooseflesh chilling a gay blade.
Real Willies, understand, don't have real bellies.
They're zombie girls who somehow die unlaid.
They fog up woodlands with a sad *ballade*
Of themselves gone begging on a damp May Eve.
A drinker caught out leaking runs himself mad

74

Once Willies breathe their symptoms up his sleeve.
He romps through *Pas de Voodoo* only his clothes leave."

XII

"*The Savage Cult of the Ungathered Rosebud*
Are we? Strange how numb she seems to our tomtoms . . ."
Careful, Gould, you're beginning to draw blood
(To my cheeks). "Your Faery Child lives in Glooms-
Ville, her eyes go up in smoke, and you bums
Puff it off in huge cloudy symbols . . ." Slump. The floor
Saw eye to eye with Gould. "When May Eve comes,"
(I propped him up) "we'll fan out in witching air,
If she sleeps, sir, she's randy, or else too cold to care."

XIII

"This *is* May Eve!" What a brilliant thrill that was!
Tom Gould, for all his whimsy, was out cold,
And I limped trembling for my brazen glass.
"Drink, Brothers, to a stark girl nineteen years old,
Who, least lecherous, with the farthest-fetched hold,
Is pulling this great fraternity's leg."
But no one's passion in the slightest cooled.
I drew beer from the almost pressureless keg,
And swore I would deliver Phi Psi from this plague.

XIV

Upstairs, Ralph was still working hard to freeze
Frenzy upon a paper dragon's snout,
His own concealing some malicious sneeze:

75

"Sure, an' it's May Eve, Bagg." Flicked his brush about,
On my lips black handlebars began to sprout.
An engine up to our preposterous wills
Stood in the cellar, groomed to smoke her out.
A phosphorescent Bike of the Baskervilles
Which soon struck bony terror through the Pelham Hills.

XV

I wheeled the great tandem, bumping upstairs,
Onto the rolling lawn. Smirking outside
Reeled the unwieldy remains of the revelers.
Ralph Lee skipped into action, sliding astride—
I, balancing the rear, worked up running speed.
Somebody sang, *Carry me to Fairy Chile,*
Belafonte coming for his brown skin bride,
But Bathurst let a Campusburp repeal
Zinner's slurs, and the scornful giggle of Dinklespiel.

XVI

We chandelled once around the Octagon
For luck, where we let feetfirst Bathurst off,
Turned left at Emily Dickinson's:
Father's house in America and all that stuff.
Far down Amity Street the dogs grew gruff,
Tooth nerves sent chilly feelers, a great house
Of tobacco gauze grew humble at a puff.
Let Chastity be reckoned gay, and who woos
Shyness be blessed. Scorn a rose with nothing to lose.

XVII

Hares thumped in our beam. We were a ghostly shiver
Down the spine of the hill plunging from Amherst
To the flat plain of the Connecticut River.
Barn owls shot rigor up our legs. Each burst
Of speed, fed to Northampton's uphill thirst
For energy, left us molasses-muscled,
Wallowing in unison, cursing this worst
Of all possible partnerships, a wild
Swan chase, pedaling human passion to a Faery Child.

XVIII

We glided through a graveyard of dead Poles.
Crickets were shilling their false pulse around
To the burrowing dead, bogged down like huge moles.
Eerie frequencies in ourselves could sound
Out tombstones just before we ran aground.
"Wake her up, rub her thighs down, Cyprian,
Make her love-crazy as an earth-bound blonde."
Ralph badgered the musty, manhandled moon
To do by magic what's oft done by telephone.

XIX

Our legs were mostly daydream by the time
White oaken columns of Greek Revival
Sailed by our elbows. Up typing a theme,
A bleary Smithie smoked at a window sill
Set in the bare pediment of that temple.
She's lonely there. New England's pulled the plug
On Zeus' parties. Her blonde whimsies can't quite fill

That niche. She welcomes with a puzzled shrug
Hephaestus knocking ashes in her Harvard mug.

x x

We dismounted to watch her wishful murals.
Those tight curls will spring and comb brown come dawn.
The slow song and dance of a girl's morals
Is what she's pouting on. Touch her, she's gone.
More hot tomato than falling star, Jack Donne.
In our glistening faces she admires herself,
Game for childbearing as the slimming moon.
Cigarette sparks scatter three stories down. "Ralph,
We're determined fellows to prefer a straight-haired Elf."

x x i

We scouted for her near Paradise Pond,
No lights on anywhere, the asylum
Imperturbable, guarding its tired blonde
Neurotics and the random mad, from some
Of the moon's harm. Moonland rolled under dorm
After dorm of soundly sleeping beauties.
That owlish typewriter pecked our tandem
To glowing bones. Fatigue had made us wise.
Who'd pedal a symbol seven miles but two Amherst guys?

x x i i

A branch or a knee unbending gently cracked.
She from the shadow of a greenhouse came,

78

Shaky and shining. Breakers must have smacked
Her ashore, shivering wet. When the moon's acclaim
Appalls her, she shies sideways, tries to comb
It from her. Something silken muffles her whoosh
Uphill, and easing in, a prancing aplomb
Plays off her hips against her breasts' soft brush
And loll under her blouse, a Queen wheeling through our hush.

XXIII

"Hooly, hooly rose she up, and here I am."
Her breath, bonny with old ballads, blew serious
Lore through our fire. "I learned in Amsterdam
Demons in highland tunes can care for us
If we deeply imagine their first caress.
The first time, I thought he had cracked my spine.
He followed me to a black slum in Paris.
I drank his burnt eyes when they shone in my wine."
Her eyes looked up, refreshed by nothing they had seen.

XXIV

"He keeps his distance now. So suave and stubborn."
She bit her lip, focusing toward her arms
A blood prince, a warrior she had shorn
Of violence after some great crimes.
"Nothing can spook him the way feline dorms
Do. When I catch myself moping down cellar
I go on long walks and show off at Proms."
Her look flicked at me from a Hitchcock thriller
Where the stunned eyes of dead nudes photograph their killer.

79

XXV

Her cheek pressed on Ralph's knee. "Strange how my phone
Was whispering delicious mysteries
Tonight. 'What talks a murmurous Latin tongue
To hale admirers? Prefers a sly tease
To a stubborn fellow careful to please?'"
"Those swine." "Oh, please, Ralph, don't be vain and silly.
That whole receiver-full of charming boys
Swore you were closing in on me, a Willi."
You have misused it, Miss Prism; please turn in your belly.

XXVI

The air grew holier as the stars set.
"Awfulest part of the experience
Comes when he leaves. He dries away like sweat.
All morning what's left of him makes me wince.
When I sleep, my body burns female incense
In his honor. He sniffs the soft things I've dreamt."
We couldn't shake her from that rambling trance.
"Sure, save me from the Devil." Why attempt
It though, unless we could match his perfect contempt?

XXVII

With an imperial flourish of disdain
Ralph kissed her hands, then landed by cartwheel
In the arms of a forlorn fountain maiden.
He set a courtly kiss on lips of steel
And basked in her strange favors for a while.
A *frisson* of deep tenderness was seeping
Through her green mossy cheekbones. Faery Child's smile

Slimmed, seeing the nymph's Victorian, safekeeping
Steel relent. She spoke, something in her voice still sleeping:

XXVIII

"There were days when that statue took exams,
The one you had a brief affair with, Ralph,
Had periods, and got hives eating clams.
(Though her father built us this unblemished sylph
She was crueler than Barbara Allen herself.)
She gave her beau the air on Saturday.
He called during Chapel with a forlorn laugh.
She sympathized in a half-hearted way.
Only a gun astonished her from being gay.

XXIX

"She galloped down the lawn to these brick stairs
And sat. For a second he seemed walking by,
Hurt deeper than she could touch with her tears.
But he stayed, smoothing the Colt on her linen thigh,
Deciding somehow she would rather die.
President Seelye's hymnal slammed, when a boom
Slammed the windows. Some girl told him why
The booms. They marched across campus and made room
For her to die in. Her killer started to walk home,

XXX

"And then he blew his own brains out. I'm willing,
Blow me apart for *that* Love, anytime.
Though I'd save him in time by turning willing.

81

Don't touch me, you *manqués,* no timid mime
Or poet armed with a phosphorescent scheme
Pleases me much. Dream up some bloodcurdling deed."
She loped off, her blink of fierce platinum
Tears tore through the harsh membranes of my pride,
The lake wind picking up her hair as she picked up speed.

XXXI

She shushed some bullfrogs and woke up an otter.
"May that tense brown kitten asleep in your lap,"
Ralph's prophecy boomed out over water,
"Scratch you to death." Our cocked ears took the slap
Of a skinspankeroo of a bellyflop.
She splashed to the far shore with vampires' hair.
"Look for no man to keep much love on tap,
Faery Child who must marry a Harvard sophomore,
A student of Zen and white writing, a wanderer."

XXXII

"Sssh, don't shout, listen to my small talk carry.
If you were closer you could see through my clothes."
All she whispered reached us warm and blurry.
"I'm going to sell my soul to the blues."
She squeezed her blouse some, and her tennis shoes
Kicked up spray, but she'd never act the befriending
Phaecian girl who gave Odysseus clothes.
We'd just cast in *that* role such an astounding
Blonde, goldsmiths' hearts for miles around would be set pound-
    ing.

XXXIII

We stood the tandem up and set her free,
Pedals frantic, ridden downhill by ghosts.
The bottom dropped out of the slope. Our spindly
Runaway splendor crashed the shifty mists
Rising from Paradise Pond. And there she rusts.
Faery Child danced below the asylum;
Massaging our eyes with dispassionate fists,
We climbed to Elm Street. Ralph with a sad thumb
Deflected all headlights that wouldn't ride us home.

XXXIV

We squeezed aboard a busty Chevrolet
Next to a rye-guzzling beatnik sophomore,
With a beard a full inch. "No shave today?"
I asked. "Don't use soap and water anymore,
Dad?" "Quiet," Ralph whispered, "He's an old timer."
His eyes invited us to his seventies.
"What are you fellows doing courtin' so late for?"
"Just chasing a honey who gave us the willies."
"Tell you, there's plenty more where she came from, laddies."

XXXV

Faery Child, plenty more where you came from?
Eve, quieting the pain in Adam's side,
Penelope, held together by a loom,
Helen, bathing in the lilyvoices of the dead,
Lucrezia, gorged on the pleasures of a bride,
Elizabeth, virgin as the New Found World,
Maud Gonne, stiff with a Grenadier's pride.

83

The splash made by wounded Zelda Fitzgerald
In the Plaza fountain—dried out next day in the New York
Herald.

Madonna of the Cello

'My child will be born soon,'
    Through a halo of her own pain.
In the warm grasp of her open thighs
    Her cello rests on the biding child.
Wakeful quintets of her senses watch
    With the restraint of angels
Over this baby that her body holds.
    She cannot touch, but heralds.

Her tiptoeing fingerings are perilously
    Leisurely,
    Docile sounds
Follow the beckons of her firm right hand.
    In strokes as surely drawn,
    Chestfilling as her breaths,
She draws out the reticent sad girl in the strings.

For women with child come by in holiness,
A donkey shall unravel winding hills
    To Bethlehem,
But this girl with her maidenhood
Scattered to the five winds of sense
    Has no comfort beyond
The wonderful body which surrounds her heart.

Her eyes may be seen as champions
    Intrigued with the war of white
And red roses in her complexion.
    Her lips bless her throat's peaceful
    Swanpale
Skin disappearing under her clothes.

She has let her hair grow
Anticipating curls,
But the strands still fall
Faithful to her neck.

From their far reaches after sadness
Her eyes look home to merry sidelong wrists,
Blue wrist veins risen,
Sinking into her fingers.

A few bars from the end
She gives in to jubilant vibrations
In the part of her that's now child.
The bow lifting from the strings
Becomes the moment after they both came,
Each falling from ecstasy
Into the other's arms.
'Some legend has gone on without us,'
Her lover said.
'Believe your tears, before they evaporate
Like notes of music from your cheeks
And your heart goes back to marking time.'
And they had sat, side
By side on the stone stairs
Of her white colonial home.
Sliding tears drew out of her eyes
The things she saw:
Her mother staring into the whorls
Of the washing machine,
Her father's eyes receding,
Her own body growing beyond her control.

Along her highstrung Puritan lineaments
    All her promises gambol again.
She nestles to the cello's gnarled flourish.
        Those doomed
    Untouchable happenings,
            Once wild,
        Soon bewildered,
Overflow her cello's rosewood curves,
    Confined to a melody
            Which aches inside her,
        Sleeps with her,
                Swells.
    It is growing into a man.

    He remembered
Her throbbing metabolism,
        When his hand reached for her shoulder,
            Lifted her breast to his passing forearm,
Almost buried her sentences in dreamy breathing,
        Carried merry water to her eyes,
            Sweat to her stomach,
        Moved her from her clothes
            Like a soul from its body:
        It now feeds her child
Bread eaten with a spirited appetite,
    Sirloin, spinach and grapefruit, her
        Particular vice,
Where the child's capillaries touch her capillaries,
    Fingers once curled restless into her lover's
        Walk on the sonata's nerves
            Singing itself to sleep.

Silence, after music, awakens the child.
Her lover opens his palm
Over her turbulent belly, where the child
Troubles it with his footprints, turning
Against the flesh.
'He was conceived when my body
Opened to you.
When my body opens to the world
He shall be born.'

Robert Bagg's writing brought him several undergraduate prizes while at Amherst College, a Simpson Fellowship for a year in Europe, and a Prix de Rome. He earned his doctorate at the University of Connecticut and has been on the faculties of the University of Washington and Smith College. He now teaches Romantic literature at the University of Massachusetts. Mr. Bagg's poetry has appeared in *Poetry, Voices, Massachusetts Review,* and *Transatlantic Review.* He has published on the history and theory of autobiographical poetry and is currently translating *Hippolytus* and *The Bacchae* of Euripides.